Boat Blokes

Peter Slater

fishing is much more than fish. It is the great occasion when we may return to the fine simplicity of our forefathers.

Herbert Hoover

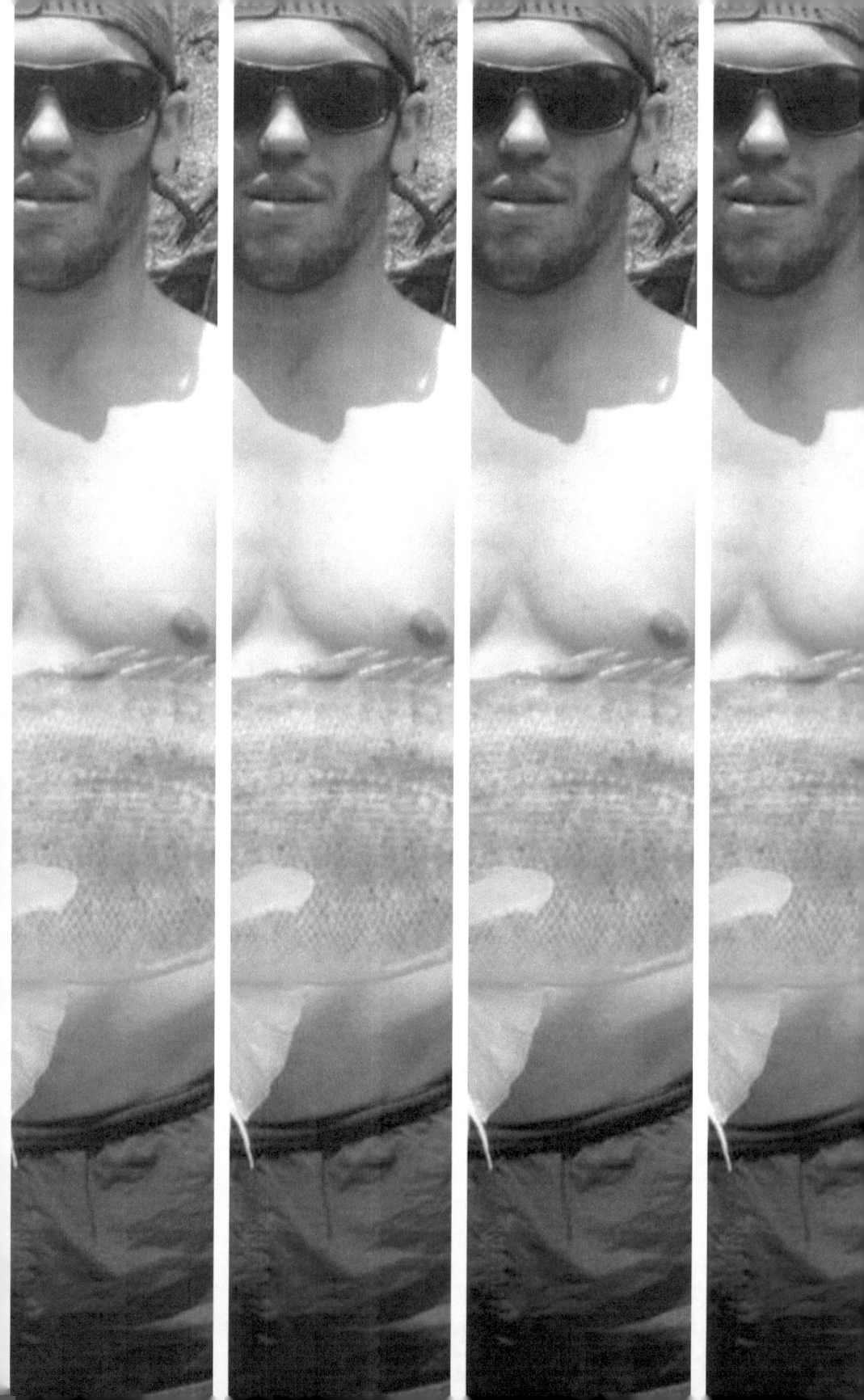

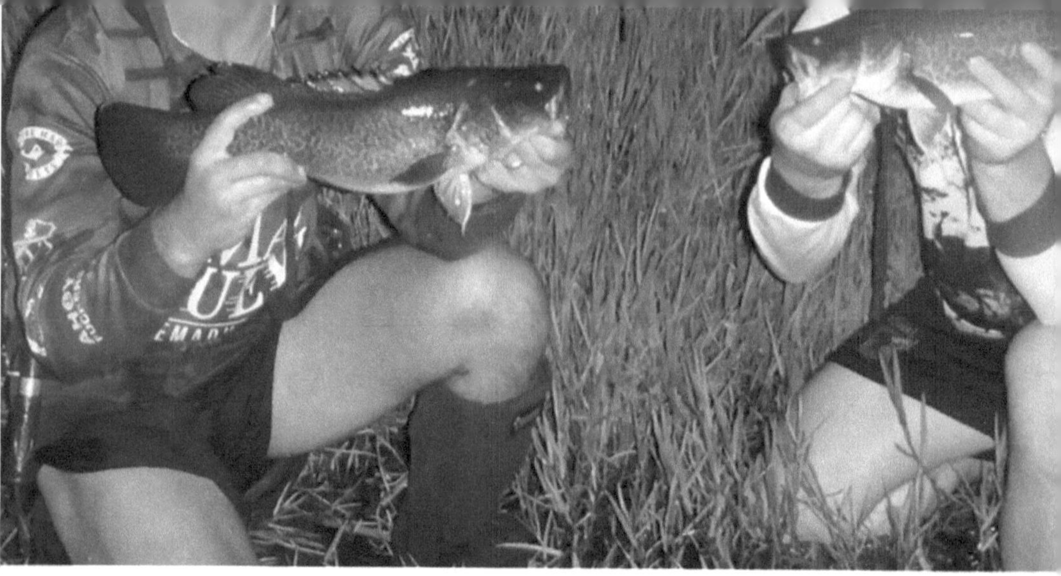

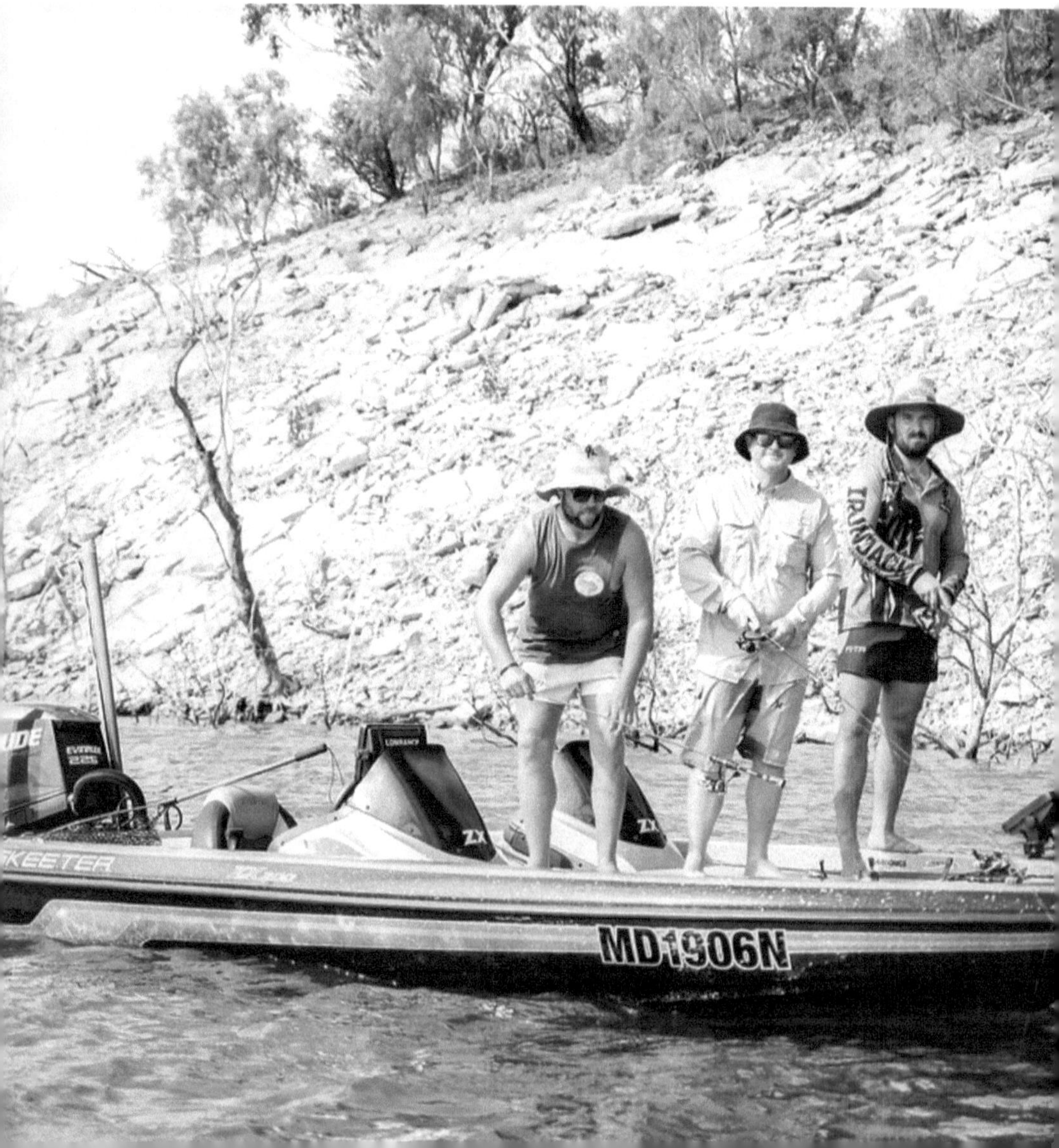
MD1906N

fishing is a hard job. fishing at night. Rain. Day, night. You have to be wise and smart. And quick.

Mariano Rivera

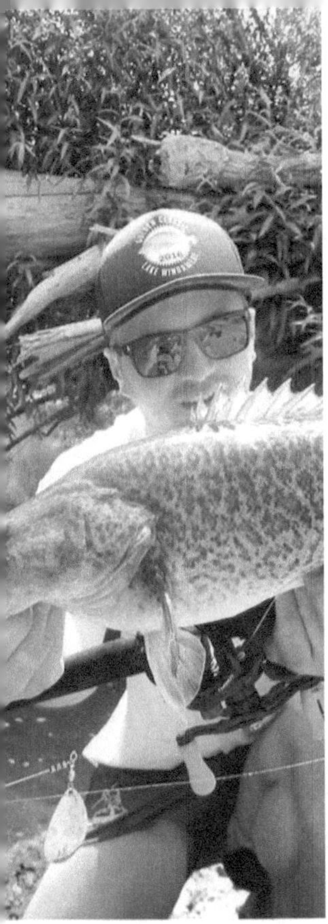

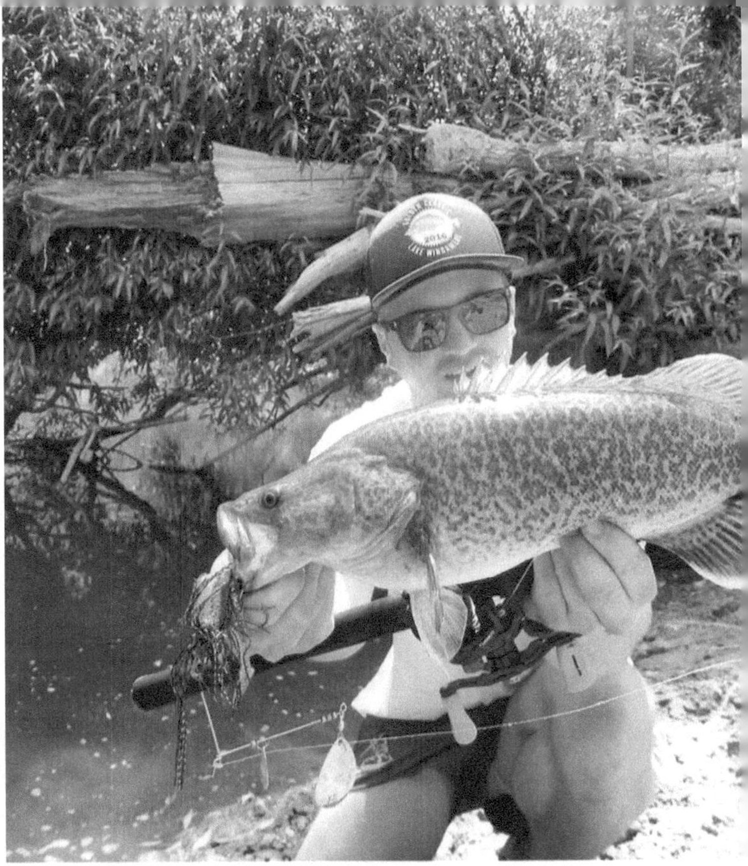

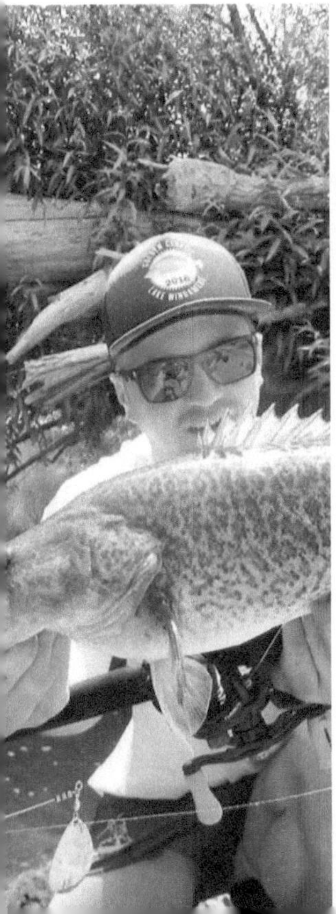

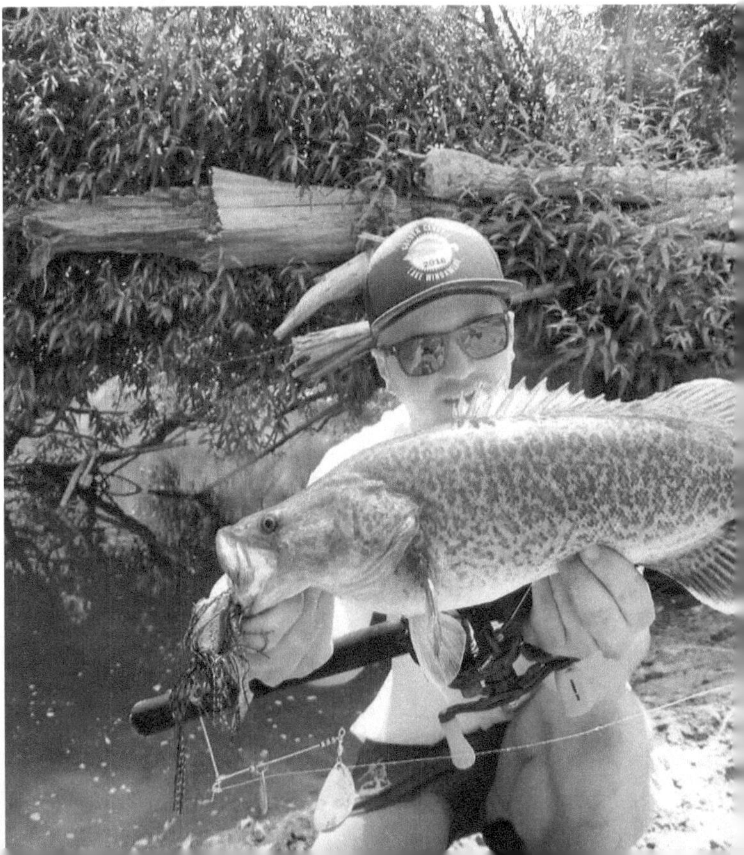

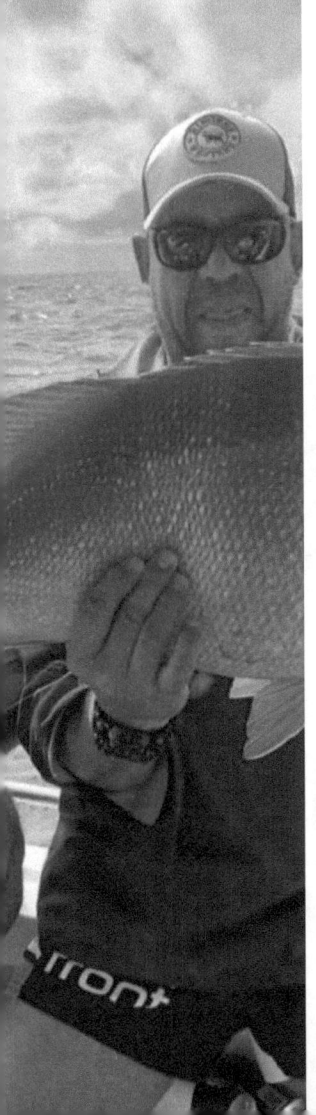

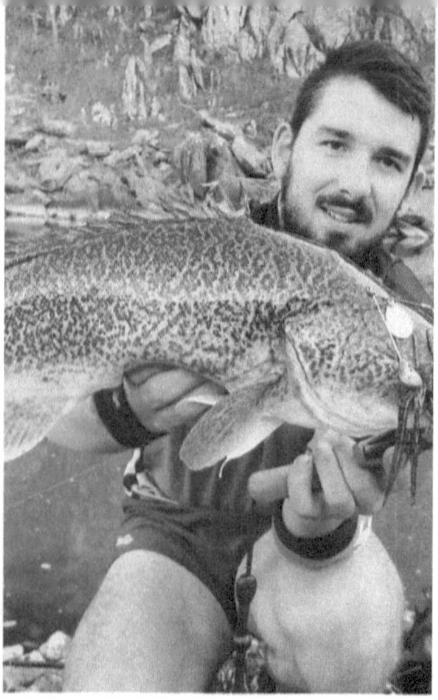
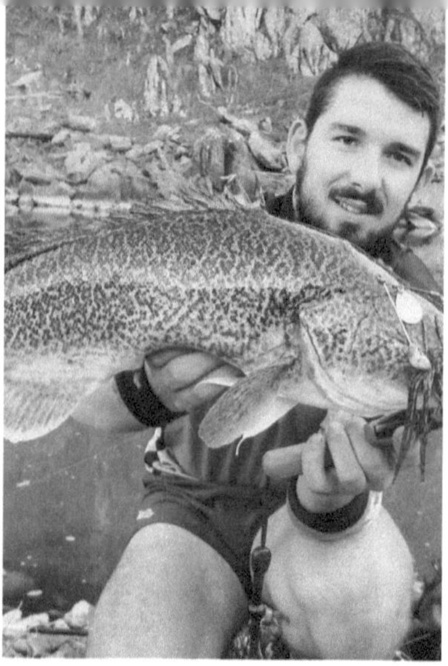
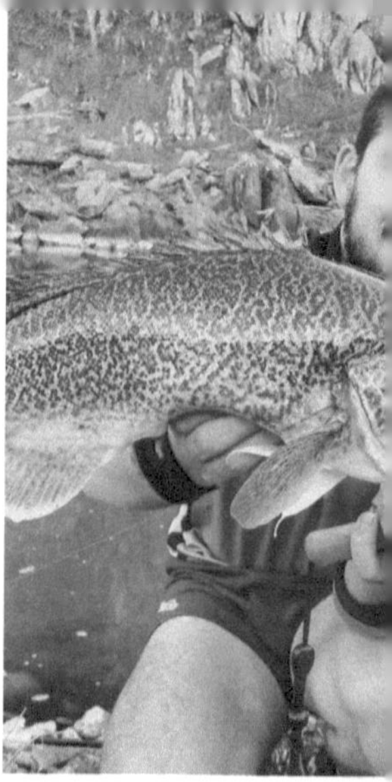
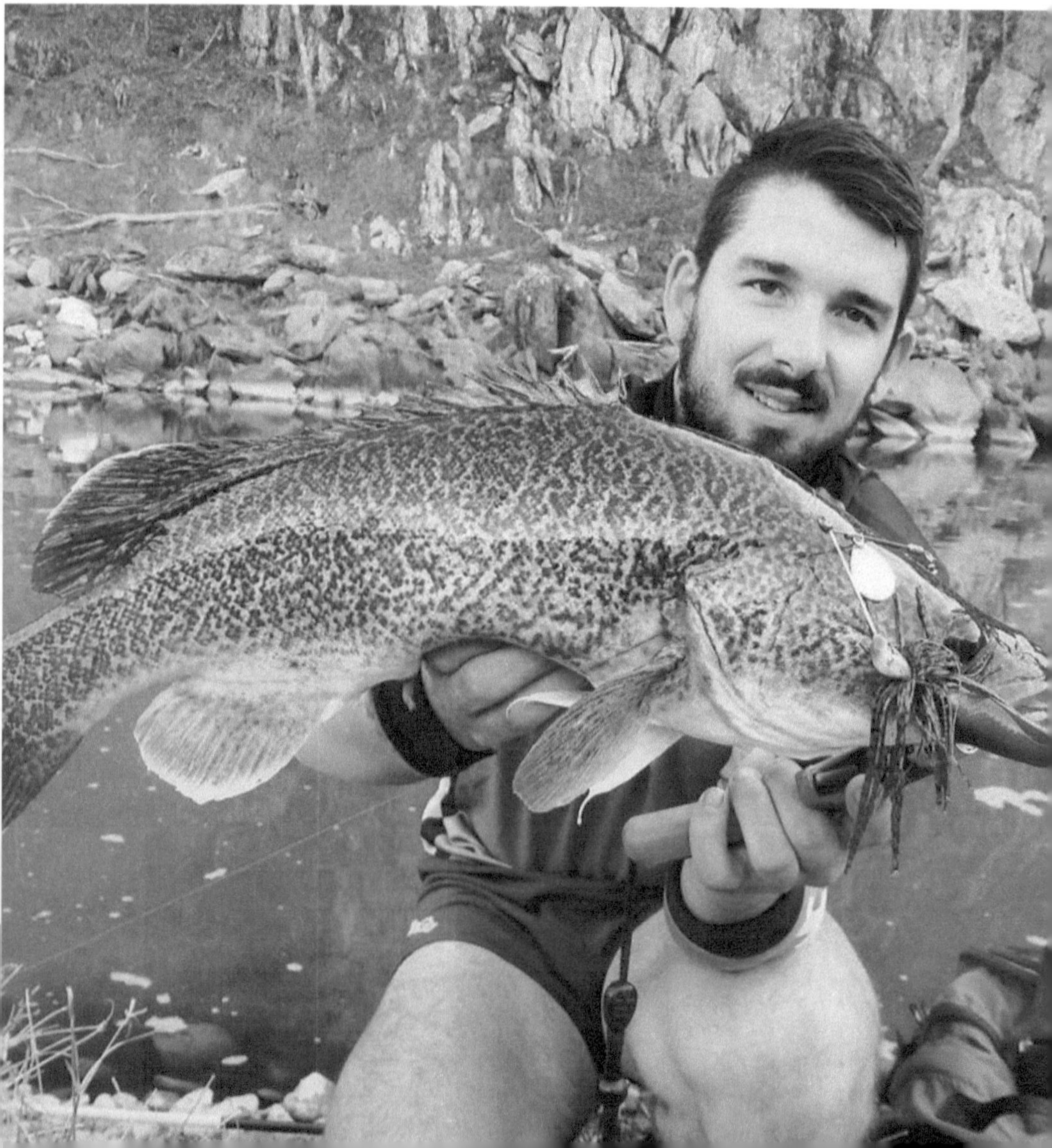

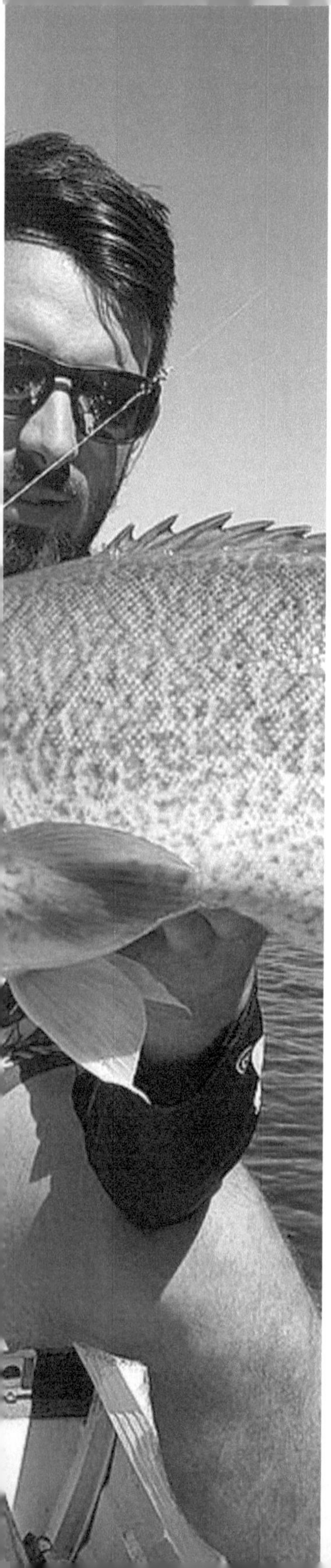

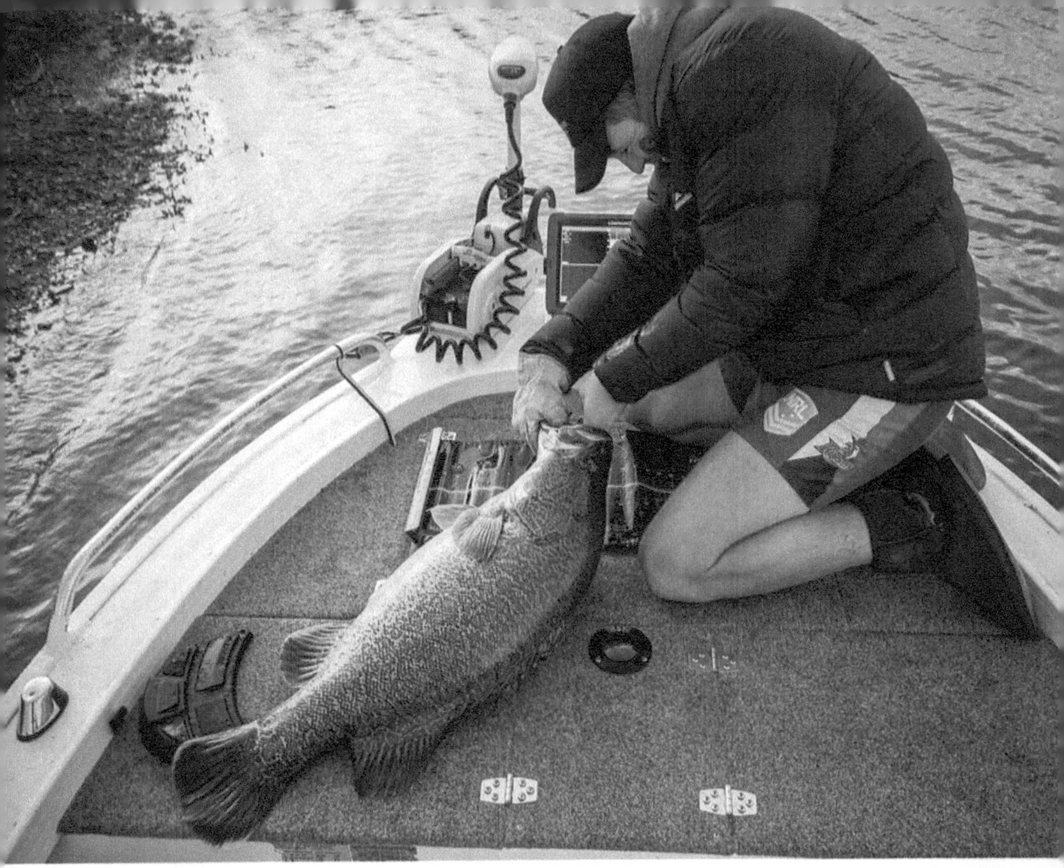

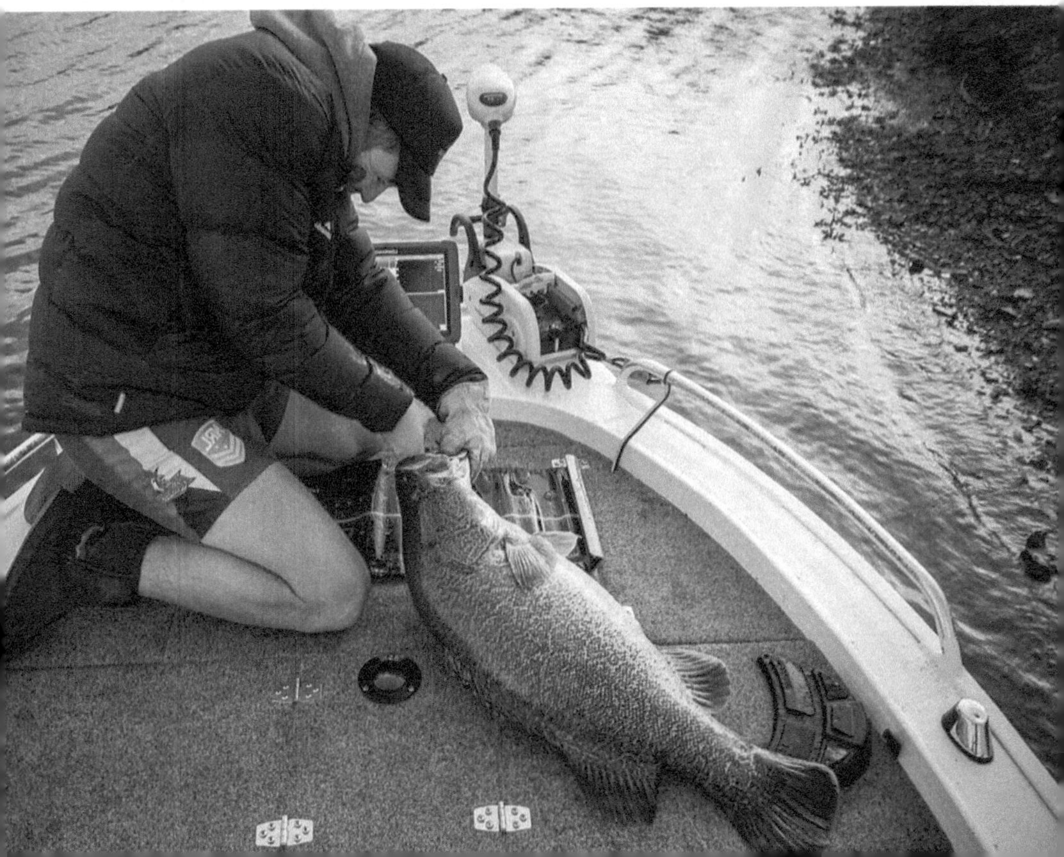

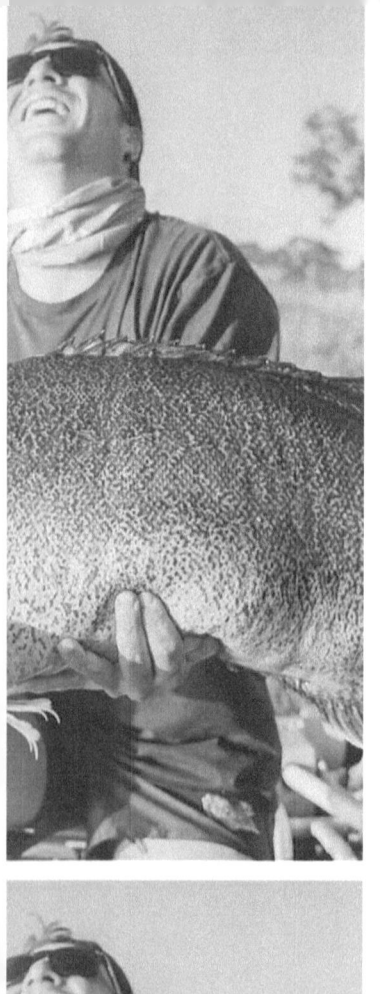

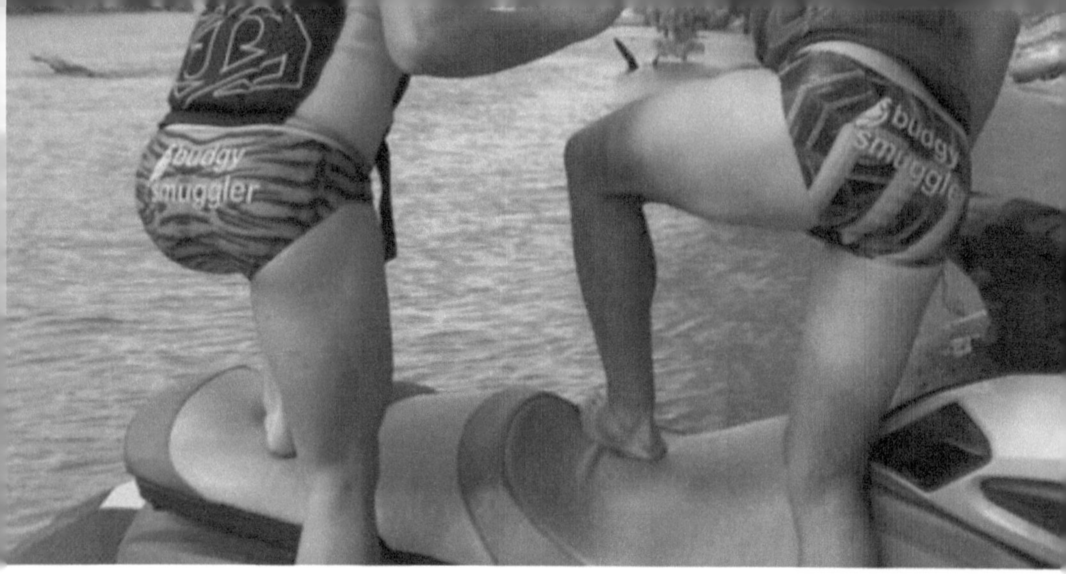
budgy
smuggler
budgy
smuggler

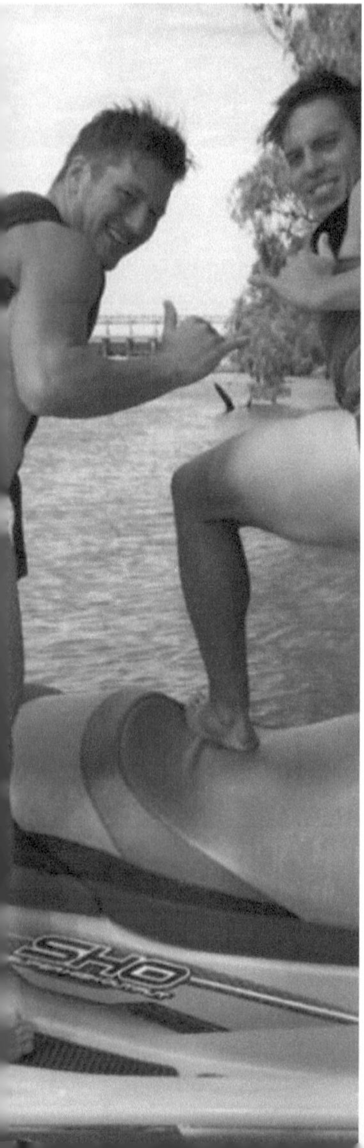
SHO

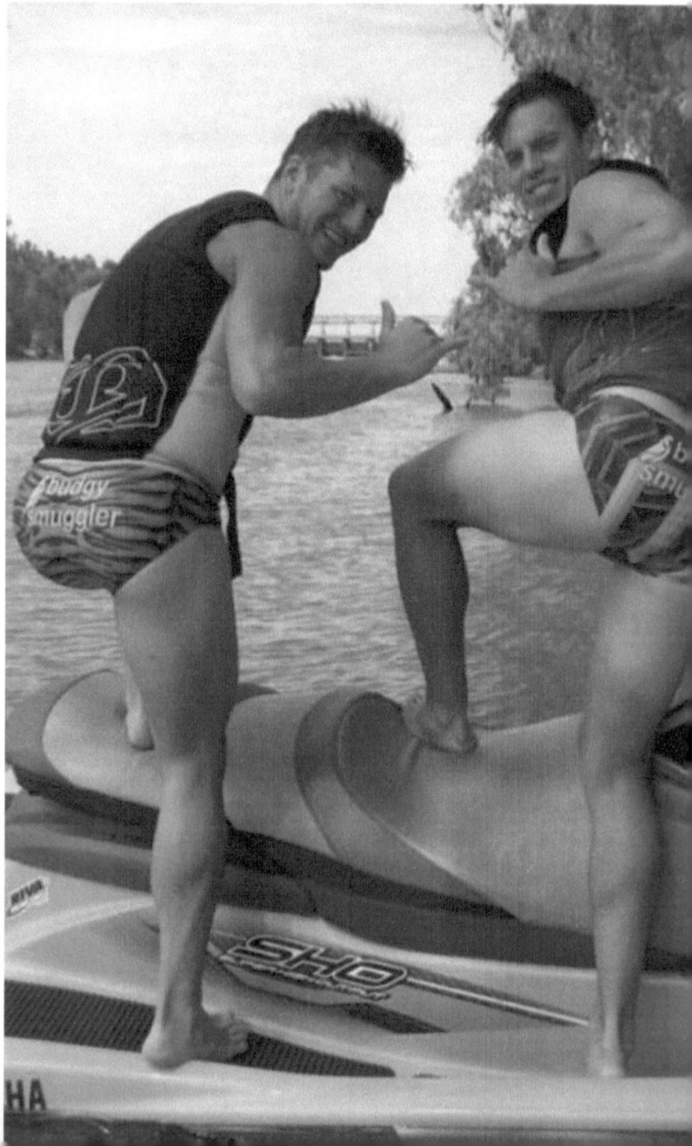
budgy
smuggler
SHO